Prancer the DEMON Chihuahua

MORE Jokes, MORE Fun!

Pam Pho

Illustrated by Cloris Chou

Andrews McMeel
PUBLISHING®

Andrews McMeel Publishing
a division of Andrews McMeel Universal
1130 Walnut Street, Kansas City, Missouri 64106

www.andrewsmcmeel.com

23 24 25 26 27 28 SDB 10 9 8 7 6 5 4 3 2 1

ISBN: 978-1-5248-7613-5

Library of Congress Control Number: 2022949424

Editor: Erinn Pascal
Art Director/Designer: Julie Barnes
Production Editor: Jennifer Straub
Production Manager: Chadd Keim

Made by:
RR Donnelley (Guangdong) Printing Solutions Co., Ltd.
Address and location of production:
No. 2 Minzhu Road, Daning, Humen Town,
Dongguan City, Guangdong Province, China 523930
1st Printing — 1/9/23

ATTENTION: SCHOOLS AND BUSINESSES
Andrews McMeel books are available at quantity discounts
with bulk purchase for educational, business, or sales
promotional use. For information, please e-mail the
Andrews McMeel Publishing Special Sales Department:
sales@amuniversal.com.

Extra, extra! Read all about it!

Hi, I'm Prancer. I'm kind of famous. It all started when my mom, Ariel, adopted me. It actually started before that, when my foster mom put me up for adoption as a "demon Chihuahua." Mom saw through that though and knew I'd make the perfect ~~overlord~~ companion for her.

Since then, I've been on the front page of the news. I've been on social media. I haven't gotten a statue in Central Bark yet, but don't worry. We're working on it.

It's kinda hard being famous.
I have to get up early. Get dressed.
Go do an interview on TV or take
photos at the studio.

On top of that, we are in the
middle of moving. I **hate** moving.

Moving means I get
less attention.

It's okay, though. If you're not getting enough attention, take a cue from me and **sing** the song of your people until you *do* get attention.

It works every time!

Five reasons why moving is the worst:

1. I am not being pampered 24/7.

2. Cardboard boxes don't taste very good.

3. The TV is already packed, so we can't watch movies.

4. My toys are also packed.

5. I don't want to go somewhere new again.

I've moved **a lot** lately.

I moved from my home into
my foster mom's house.
Then I moved in with Ariel.
Now we are moving **again.**

I will have to find a new walkies route. What if my new neighborhood doesn't have a coffee shop that makes **puppuccinos?**

WHAT IF MY NEW NEIGHBORHOOD DOESN'T HAVE A PLACE TO BUY BACON, EGG, AND CHEESE SANDWICHES?!

Bacon, egg, and cheese sandwiches are my absolute **favorite.**

Nothing is as cheesy, greasy, or bacon-y as them.

NOTHING!

I do **NOT** like packing my things to move them to a new place that I don't even know anything about.

The **moving van** is here.
Time to go. I guess…

Goodbye, gorgeous walkies!

Adios, Mom's closet!

Sayonara, the first place I . . .
ever felt at **home.**

And "hello" to new.

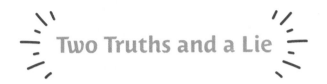

Two Truths and a Lie

I will tell you two true things and one lie.
Let's see if you can guess the lie correctly.

1. I've modeled dog clothing on a runway in Paris.

2. I have been given an award by a mayor in Connecticut.

3. The first thing I did in the new house was pee on the front room carpet.

Did you guess #1? Then you are correct! I can't give you any awards like the mayor, so give yourself a walkie as a reward.

The only good thing about moving is a **new** place to mark my territory.

And the **couch** is still okay.

Fine. I guess there's some good things about moving into a new place.

For example, the walls.

They're all me.

Like it should be.

And my closet is **bigger** here, too, which is good, because I need a place to store all my clothes.

This is important because when I'm **uber famous,** I'll need even more clothes.

I know I'm kinda famous now, but I have plans. Big plans! I want to make sure Chihuahuas get a better rap everywhere.

Sure, we may be small, and okay, we may sometimes be mean, but there's also a sweet side to us. *Sometimes.* Just look at these cute Chihuahua eyes!

And you know how people say there's "cat people" and "dog people" out there? Well, "Chihuahua people" are just **different.**

I can't wait until the world is FULL OF CHIHUAHUA PEOPLE.

But first I gotta get uber famous. See, when you're uber famous, you also get to enact some fun things. Like...

TOP TEN THINGS I AM GONNA CHANGE WHEN I AM UBER FAMOUS:

1. All dog food now tastes like bacon, egg, and cheese.

2. All cats are to live in bathtubs. This is so dogs never have to get bathed again.

3. Tech leaders will drop everything to find a way for dogs and humans to communicate. (Less for humans to communicate, and more for dogs to BARK ORDERS!)

4. All books about cats must immediately change to being about dogs.

5. The coffee shop will open a location in my home.

6. "Hollywood" will change its name to "Doggywood" and all dogs—but especially Chihuahuas—will get wooden sticks to chew on when they visit. Souvenirs!

7. Dogs will reign supreme, but Chihuahuas will be #1.

8. Since uber famous dogs can do whatever they want, I will become President of the United States.

9. Then I'll become President of the World ... because why not.

10. When I am President of the World, all cats will relocate from bathtubs to Australia. (Sorry, Australia.)

For my first State of the Union Address as President, I will cover some huge topics. Here's what I have written so far:

Thank you, citizens, for electing me as your President. I have lived in the United States my entire life. I believe that makes me qualified to run our illustrious country. From now on all cats will be relocated to bathtubs. If you would like to remain with your cat, you can. However, that means you must live in a bathtub. This is important because dogs should not have baths ever. ESPECIALLY not when soap gets in our eyes...ugh.

All coffee shops are to begin serving large puppuccinos, or pup cups, to all dogs immediately and for free. Chihuahuas get extra-large pup cups because Chihuahuas are the best.

There will be no war because we are the land of bacon, egg, and cheese. We, as a nation, need to move on from our past political mistakes and focus solely on bacon, egg, and cheese. The price of bacon will now be the foundation of our economy.

Please line up at your local shelter and assume responsibility for your new furever friend beginning at 9 a.m. tomorrow.

Thank you, America.

Oh, also, there will be a **National Chihuahua Day.**

Apparently, that already exists and it's on May 14th.

But, under my uber famous rule, National Chihuahua Day will be EVERY DAY, and occasionally it'll be National PRANCER THE DEMON CHIHUAHUA DAY. I'd make Prancer Day every day, but I want to give my fans something to look forward to.

Speaking of something to look forward to ...

I think Ariel has noticed that I'm sad about the new house.

It's all the same furniture but in a new place. It just doesn't feel like home.

So today she's taking me ... ON OUR NEW WALKIE ROUTE!

Smells … smelly.

These smells are even **better**.

A Haiku About Pup Cups

I love you, pup cup
You are so light and airy
I am a huge fan

(**Did you know?** Haikus are special poems that have a different and specific number of syllables in each line. The first line has five syllables. The second line has seven syllables. The third line has five syllables again.

Have you ever written a haiku? I bet it's not as good as mine, but you can try.)

Unfortunately, Ariel has told me that dogs can't be President. There's some rule against it or whatever. **Booooooring.**

I'd rock the wig.

That's okay, though. I have a new goal to be UBER FAMOUS. I'm going to be a movie star.

Quiz: What should the plot of my movie be?

1. ***Ruff 'n Rumble:*** An action movie! Prancer is a Chihuahua who lives in Philadelphia and has to learn street-fighting to buy Mom a house.

2. ***Feline Failure:*** A sci-fi flick! Prancer is on a mission to eradicate the world's cat population. (AKA, put them all in Australia—except in this movie, Australia is on THE MOON. You know. For science.)

3. ***Milan Model:*** A rom-com romp! Prancer is a famous fashion model that creates his own clothing line and falls in love with his makeup artist.

Answer: All of them. Doggywood, call this Chihuahua already!

And in case that doesn't work out,
I can always be a **musician.**

Or become uber famous by being
the first Chihuahua on **Mars.**

PRANCER!!!

Heh. I think Mom found that pee I made earlier...

Time for a quiz break.

You might not be kinda famous like me, but that's okay, you can work your way up there. Find out just how legendary you are with this super fun quiz!

1. **Do you like poetry?**
   a. Yes
   b. No

2. **Do you like social media?**
   a. Yes
   b. No

3. **Do you like fashion?**
   a. Yes
   b. No

4. **Do you like sandwiches?**
   a. Yes
   b. No

5. **Do you love bacon?**
   a. Yes
   b. No

Now count how many a's you circled to find your answer!

1–2 a's
What? Maybe you're a cat.

2–3 a's
You're getting there, but you need to model some more clothing. Get out there and work it!

4–5 a's
You have unleashed your inner demonic Chihuahua and are the champion of sending cats to the bathtub (or Australia. Or space). Congrats! Let's be friends.

One place I feel uber famous at is my grandma's house. My grandma is my mom's mom, but that doesn't matter because she's *my* grandma. Do you have someone that makes you feel **special?** Well, it can't be my grandma, because she's taken.

Mom says that I have to stay at grandma's house for a few days. Mom is having surgery and *apparently* dogs can't be in the operating room. *Apparently* Mom can't go for walks with me after surgery, either. This surgery stuff bites.

You know what? Maybe I'll just become an **UBER FAMOUS doctor** and re-write those rules! Now, whenever humans get surgery, they get THREE CHIHUAHUAS with it! (I call it: ChihuahuaCare!)

This human must adopt a chihuahua, love the chihuahua forever, and give them lots of bacon, egg, and cheese sandwiches. Signed,

PrancerDemon
MD

Apparently, some dogs kind of ARE doctors; there are **service dogs,** who are trained to perform tasks for their handler, and therapy dogs, who help people cope with stuff like PTSD (post-traumatic stress disorder), anxiety, and depression.

Therapy and service dogs sound awesome. And I think we could all use a little therapy.

Maybe that's something I'd enact as PRESIDENT OF THE WORLD. Therapy for all! Chihuahuas for all! Good luck and good night.

*Service dogs and therapy dogs are different. Service dogs help a certain person with a disability complete tasks. Therapy dogs provide support too, but to a wider group than their specific handler.

Mom is on **bed rest** for a few days.
That means she has to stay in bed.

I *love* bed rest.

I wish we could do this all the time!

I guess I don't mind "couch rest," either.

Or "armrest."

Okay, maybe I just like **rest.**

Maybe I'll be an UBER FAMOUS inventor.

Here's some inventions that I think we could really use.

Uber Famous-Worthy Inventions
BY: PRANCER

1. **A cat translator.** They probably don't say anything interesting, but now you can yell at cats in "Cat."

2. **A dog translator.** We say lots of interesting things, and this will *definitely* come in handy when everyone in the world has a Chihuahua.

3. **Bacon, egg, and cheesecakes.** Okay, hear me out on this one. Bacon, egg, and cheese sandwiches are delicious. Cheesecakes are delicious. Yes, I'll be trademarking the idea—"marking" means "peeing on it," right?

4. **A dig robot.** I love digging as much as the next pup, but a robot that can do it *for* you? I'm in.

5. **Squirrel bait.** This baits *only* squirrels, so that you can make them come over and then chase them.

6. **A *squirrel translator***... I guess. I don't think squirrels have interesting things to say, either. But you could yell, "HEY SQUIRREL, LET ME CHASE YOU" at it, so that's probably good enough to make me uber famous.

7. **A *never-ending litterbox*.** This one is really to relieve Australia of cats once I'm President of the World. If cats had a never-ending litterbox, they'd probably be happy or whatever and Australia's wombat population can be happy too.

8. **A *wombat translator?*** Okay, I just looked it up, and wombats are kinda cute. They probably say interesting things.

9. **ic *Fashionable clothing for dogs*** that doesn't make us want to bite them. Sometimes it's instinct and you must bite. But this way, dogs everywhere will look fashionable and RESIST THE URGE.

10. **A *blanket*** that's not too cold and not too soft. It actually changes temperatures according to what you want, because it's a cool invention made by an uber famous inventor, and we can do stuff like that.

I LOVE PRANCER THE DEMON CHIHUAHUA.

Time for another haiku!

I am in love with
Mornings, the air is crispy
Shut those birds up please

I could be an **uber famous** poet.

If I want to be seen as a serious poet,
I need to up my game and write many
different kinds of poetry.

Poets get fancy feather pens.

Prancer's First Sonnet*
by: Prancer

Let us speak to the woes of moving
Admit that it is the worst
Change alters, to change I am booing
Of new walkies routes and stores:
I am not a fan,
That pet store on the new high street;
Filled with clothing not couture,
Know that my needs you will never meet.
The café is okay and the owner kind
I am not satisfied with these delights;
I feel a deep sadness inside of my mind,
But with change comes excitement.
I am with my mom and that is great,
I never once doubted I am loved.

* Sonnets are poems with fourteen lines. Fourteen is also the amount
of bacon, egg, and cheese sandwiches it takes to please me.

Top Five Places to Be Petted

(Don't ask when. The answer is ALWAYS.)

1. My ears. A great ear rub is hard to find.

2. My belly. Unless you tickle me. Do not tickle me.

3. Under my chin, but don't talk about my second chin.

4. Slow circles on top of my head.

5. Bootie. Butt. Scritches.

HERE

HERE

NOT HERE

ESPECIALLY HERE

HERE

If you pet a Chihuahua in their favorite spot, you might see the pup do the **LEG THING.** It's when we get so excited, we can't stop shaking our leg. It's a true honor!

Oh, sorry.

I think I got some of my **bacon, egg, and cheese sandwich** on this page.

Just ... ignore this, okay?

Or take a sandwich break.

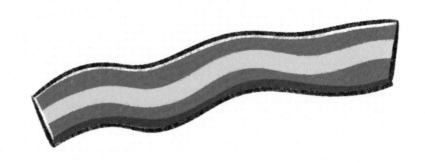

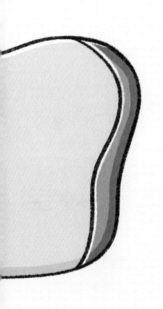

Story time!

Mom and I were trying out a new walkie route when we saw a woman walking her CAT.

CATS SHOULD NOT BE ON LEASHES. THAT IS DOGS ONLY.

As if that wasn't bad enough, this lady walked up and gushed to Mom about how cute I am.

Like, dude, we know I am cute. She then proceeded to tell Mom that I have an "11 out of 10" boopable nose. I gave her my best "try me, Karen" look.

She started reaching toward me. Mom tensed, which let me know she did not want me to be touched either. I decided to bark and show a little teeth. Karen freaked out and screamed that I am evil.

I'm not evil, though. Just a little demonic.

The lady was right though—I do have a pretty boopable nose.

11 out of 10 boopable

Royal Decree By Prancer, Uber Famous Chihuahua

All people named Karen must
move to Australia, too.

(This is nothing against Australia, by the
way. I happen to like Australian accents
and the way Australians say "Prancer."
But Australia IS far from where I live,
so that's where cats and Karens go.)

I also think I'd like **kangaroos.**

But I digress!

Something I don't like?

Whatever this is. Mom calls it going to the "VET." Probably stands for **Very Excruciating Trip**. But Mom says my stomach has been grumbling lately. (I mean, duh, there's an obvious lack of bacon, egg, and cheese sandwiches in it.)

Oh, yeah. I guess I **did** eat
Mom's ear bud.

In my defense, an ear bud
looks kind of like a jelly bean.

VET BILL $600

Dear reader, I did not, in fact, poop it out.

I guess I *have* to become **uber famous** now to pay Mom back.

New idea: motivational speaking!

GIVING

WHEN YOU GIVE MORE, YOU GET MORE.

You are into fitness. I am into fit'n'iss cheddar **cheeseburger** into my mouth.

Motivational Advice from Prancer, the Uber Famous Demon Chihuahua

1. We cannot solve problems if we are the drama.

2. Live as if you are alive.

3. Money doesn't grow happiness, but cheese does, and you can buy cheese with money.

4. Cheese that goes uneaten is cheese wasted.

5. You need a chicken if you want eggs.

6. Your career shouldn't dictate your life. You have a dog for that.

7. You can squeeze the orange to make juice, but you can just buy juice at the store.

8. Think, breathe, and act like a dog.

Another Haiku From Me

I'm a Chihuahua
With love and anxiety
Please keep boundaries

Apparently, the uber famous
don't get **boundaries.**

Maybe I don't want to be uber
famous anymore . . .

As a kinda famous Chihuahua, I can **blend in**—NO, not like that blender! C'mon, what were you thinking?!

Quiz time!

1. **If you could be only one, which would you choose?**
   a. A movie star
   b. A famous author
   c. A supermodel
   d. A Chihuahua

2. **Where do you want to live?**
   a. A warm beach town
   b. Cold mountains
   c. A bustling city
   d. In a forest near a river

3. **What do you want to eat right now?**
   a. Spaghetti
   b. Cheeseburger
   c. BLT
   d. Cake

4. What kind of pet do you want?

   a. A dog

   b. A cat

   c. A bird

   d. The king of beasts, a Chihuahua

Okay, there's no answers for this quiz. But I am 100% judging you by your answers. The ink you just used uploaded your answers into my brain. I know what you picked ...

Judging **YOU.**

(You didn't say "cat" on that last question, right? Because ... after all of this, that would be kinda weird.)

Anyway.

What's **NOT WEIRD** is how good
I am at modeling clothing.

Here's some of my favorite pieces!

Simple **basics,** like this red hoodie.

A **fashionable** fur. *Faux fur. Faux!*

A simple, **crisp** sweater.

You know, maybe the *kinda famous* life is right for me.

It means I can stay all day in Grandpa's lap.

I don't usually like dudes, but I love Grandpa.

And there's no better meal on earth than what Grandma can make. Her bacon, egg, cheese, and potato casserole is probably my **favorite thing** on this planet.

I'm going to make a goal list and manifest it into being. I read all about manifesting in *Opawulance Magazine*.

Manifesting:

It's thinking about what you want and encouraging the **Universe** to make it happen for you.

I'm manifesting
CHIHUAHUAS
getting a better rap.

Bacon, egg, and cheese sandwiches.

And therapy for all!

Next year, I want:

1. To be the spokesperson of bacon

2. To be the owner of a HUGE block of fancy French cheese

3. To make this book a *New Bark Times* bestseller

4. To model tons more clothes

5. To pay Mom back for that vet bill ... I guess, and ...

6. CHIHUAHUA WORLD DOMINATION

Now, I'll work on being my **best self** and making my goals happen!

nama-STAY

Just remember.

Chihuahuas are the **best.**

Smell you later!

I want to thank **Second Chance Pet Rescue** for finding my new mom and taking care of me when I didn't have a home. I'd also like to thank cheese, squirrels, bacon, and cheeseburgers.

I want to thank Tyfanee Fortuna, Prancer's foster mom, for choosing me to adopt him. A huge thank you to Last Chance Adoption for helping animals like Prancer find homes. Most importantly, I'd like to thank Prancer. He has challenged me every day to be the best version of myself and I don't know what I'd do without him.

Ariel

I want to thank Prancer for bringing so much light into the world during a pandemic. I'd also like to thank Ariel, his mom, for trusting me to write this book and help spread the love of Prancer even farther. I haven't met a more patient and kind editor than Erinn Pascal. She guided Ariel, Prancer, and I through this process and made this book so much more fun. I'd like to thank the team at Andrews McMeel for taking care of us and being so involved in this process. Cloris, your illustrations made everything so much brighter. You are a true artist. I'd like to thank my mom and my step-dad for letting me read constantly. To my husband Brandon and my children Addie and Elijah, thank you for reading this during every revision and helping me make better jokes. To Dolly Parton for starting the Imagination Library. A very special thank you to my elementary school librarian Ms. White: you gave a young farm girl the gift of reading and that lasted a lifetime.

Pam